Nature Schoo

LET'S LOOK FOR LEAVES!

By Seth Lynch

Gareth Stevens
PUBLISHING

Please visit our website, www.garethstevens.com. For a free color catalog of all our high-quality books, call toll free 1-800-542-2595 or fax 1-877-542-2596.

Library of Congress Cataloging-in-Publication Data

Names: Lynch, Seth, author.
Title: Let's look for leaves! / Seth Lynch.
Description: Buffalo, New York : Gareth Stevens Publishing, [2024] |
    Series: Nature school | Includes index. | Audience: Grades K-1
Identifiers: LCCN 2022045112 (print) | LCCN 2022045113 (ebook) | ISBN
    9781538286272 (library binding) | ISBN 9781538286258 (paperback) | ISBN
    9781538286845 (ebook other)
Subjects: LCSH: Leaves–Juvenile literature.
Classification: LCC QK649 .L96 2024 (print) | LCC QK649 (ebook) | DDC
    581.4/8–dc23/eng/20220927
LC record available at https://lccn.loc.gov/2022045112
LC ebook record available at https://lccn.loc.gov/2022045113

First Edition

Published in 2024 by
Gareth Stevens Publishing
2544 Clinton St,
Buffalo, NY 14224

Copyright © 2024 Gareth Stevens Publishing

Editor: Kristen Nelson
Designer: Claire Wrazin

Photo credits: Cover ArTDi101/Shutterstock.com; p. 1 imnoom/Shutterstock.com; p. 5 BalanceFormCreative/Shutterstock.com; p. 7 Ryzhkov Oleksandr/Shutterstock.com; p. 9 Det-anan/Shutterstock.com; pp. 11, 24 (right) Fotofermer/Shutterstock.com; pp. 13, 24 (left) kzww/Shutterstock.com/Shutterstock.com; p. 13 (arrow) Lyudmyla Ishchenko/Shutterstock.com; pp. 15, 24 (middle) sichkarenko.com/Shutterstock.com; p. 17 Kokhanchikov/Shutterstock.com; p. 19 Bayhu19/Shutterstock.com; p. 21 Elena Elisseeva/Shutterstock.com; p. 23 Pamela Weston/Shutterstock.com

Printed in the United States of America

CPSIA compliance information: Batch #CS24GS: For further information contact Gareth Stevens, New York, New York at 1-800-542-2595.

Find us on

Contents

Let's look for leaves!

Leaves are part of plants.
They may join to a stem.

We see tulip leaves.
They are long
and green.

Leaves may have
a stalk.
This joins a branch.

We see an oak tree.
Its leaves have parts.
These are lobes.

Pine trees have needles.
These are small leaves.

Leaves help plants make food.
They take in sunlight, water, and air.

We see a sunflower.
Its leaves look like
a heart.

We see a maple tree.
Its leaves are green now.

They change color
in fall!

Words to Know

lobe   needles   stalk

Index